Compliments of

Canada
FOCUS
ON THE FAMILY

Helping families thrive

Website: www.focusonthefamily.ca
Toll free: 1-800-661-9800

Presented to

_____

by

_____

on

_____

ZONDERKIDZ

God's Messages for Little Ones
Copyright © 2012 by Max Lucado, Randy Frazee, Karen Davis Hill
Illustrations © 2012 by Josée Masse

Requests for information should be addressed to:
Zonderkidz, 5300 Patterson Ave. SE, Grand Rapids, Michigan 49530

ISBN 978-0-310-73292-1

All Scripture quotations, unless otherwise indicated, are taken from the Holy Bible,
New International Version®, NIrV®. Copyright © 1973, 1978, 1984, 2011 by Biblica, Inc.™
Used by permission of Zondervan. All rights reserved worldwide.

Any Internet addresses (websites, blogs, etc.) and telephone numbers in this book are
offered as a resource. They are not intended in any way to be or imply an endorse-
ment by Zondervan, nor does Zondervan vouch for the content of these sites and
numbers for the life of this book.

All rights reserved. No part of this publication may be reproduced, stored in a
retrieval system, or transmitted in any form or by any means — electronic, mechanical,
photocopy, recording, or any other — except for brief quotations in printed reviews,
without the prior permission of the publisher.

Published in association with Steve Green and Anvil.

Zonderkidz is a trademark of Zondervan.

Editor: Mary Hassinger
Design: Cindy Davis

Printed in China

12 13 14 15 16 17 /LPC/ 6 5 4 3 2 1

31 DEVOTIONS

GOD'S MESSAGES
FOR LITTLE ONES

THE STORY OF GOD'S ENORMOUS LOVE

Max Lucado, Randy Frazee, Karen Davis Hill
Illustrations by Josée Masse

Jesus said, "Let the little children come to me.
Don't keep them away. The Kingdom of heaven
belongs to people like them."

—Matthew 19:14

ZONDER**k**i**d**z

ZONDERVAN.com/
AUTHORTRACKER
follow your favorite authors

Contents

Day 1

"God saw everything he had made.
And it was very good."

Genesis 1:31a

God made Adam and Eve.
God made me too.
It feels great to be a child of God!

GOD SAYS TO ME ...

You are my greatest creation.
Looking at you is better than
looking at an ocean view.
Watching you run and play is better
than watching beautiful animals
dart across the African plain.
Seeing a smile on your face is
better than seeing a sunrise.
You are my pride and joy.

Day 2

"Abram believed the Lord. The Lord
accepted Abram because he believed. So
his faith made him right with the Lord."

Genesis 15:6

Abraham trusted God.
I can trust God too.
He will always love me.

GOD SAYS TO ME …

I will be your God forever and ever.
You and your relatives will be my
special people. My blessings will be
with you and your children and
your children's children through a
thousand generations.

Day 3

"We know that in all things God works for
the good of those who love him."

Romans 8:28

❧

God took care of Joseph.
God takes care of me.
He takes care of my family too.

GOD SAYS TO ME …

No matter where you go,
I am with you. Nothing can
separate you from my love.
I am your God and you are my child.
Always remember that when
you trust me with your life,
I will do great things through you.

Day 4

"They will know that I am the
Lord their God."

Exodus 29:46

❧

God watched over Moses.
He watched over his people.
God watches over me too.

GOD SAYS TO ME ...

I am your Father,
watching over you night and day.
I will love you and protect you
wherever you go,
even when you think things
are impossible.

Day 5

"Moses went and told the people all of the Lord's words and laws. They answered with one voice. They said, 'We will do everything the Lord has told us to do.'"

Exodus 24:3

A long time ago, God gave his people ten special rules to follow. These rules are for me too.

GOD SAYS TO ME …

Let my grace guide your words
and actions. You are my people,
my chosen ones.
You are my child.
I have set you apart from all
other nations. Be a shining
example wherever you go.

Day 6

"I, the Lord, have spoken."
Numbers 14:35

❧

God has kept all of his promises.
He keeps his promises to me too.

GOD SAYS TO ME ...

One day you will have faith in me.
One day you will trust me to take
care of your every need.
One day you will love me with
all your heart as I love you.
When that day comes
you will find peace.

Day 7

**"I am the Lord your God. I will be with
you everywhere you go."**

Joshua 1:9

God loves his people.
He gives his people help.
I can be a helper too.

GOD SAYS TO ME ...

You are my chosen people!
Rejoice in your victory.
And let my name be known
among the nations
that I am the one true God,
and you are my chosen people!
You are mine and I love you.

Day 8

"Then he prayed to the Lord. He said,
'Lord and King, show me that you still
have concern for me. God, please make
me strong just one more time'."

Judges 16:28a

~

Samson asked God to help him.
I can ask God for help too.

GOD SAYS TO ME ...

I am God Almighty.
My strength shines
through the leader of my people.
Call on me and I will answer.
I will use my power to help you.

Day 9

"Where you go I'll go.
Where you stay I'll stay."

Ruth 1:16

Ruth was kind.
Boaz was kind.
God smiles when I am kind.

GOD SAYS TO ME …

I have chosen you for a journey.
Trust in my plan. Just like I had
a job for Ruth, Naomi, and Boaz,
I have a special job for you.
Be kind and know that
you make me happy.

Day 10

"The Lord has given me
what I asked him for."
1 Samuel 1:27b

God heard Hannah's prayer.
He heard Samuel's prayer.
God hears my prayers too.

GOD SAYS TO ME ...

Be still and listen,
I am calling your name.
I have chosen you.
Through you, people will
hear my words and follow me.

Day 11

"Man looks at how someone appears on the outside. But I look at what is in the heart."

1 Samuel 16:7b

❧

God helped young David be brave.
If I ask, God will help me be brave too.

GOD SAYS TO ME ...

I have chosen you
not for your riches
or your name
or for how you look.
I have chosen you for your
tenderness and kindness.
I love your good heart. Be brave.

Day 12

"God, create a pure heart in me. Give me
a new spirit that is faithful to you."

Psalm 51:10

God forgave David.
God will forgive me.
I will tell him I am sorry.

GOD SAYS TO ME ...

Your song of praise
rises sweetly to the heavens.
My heart is filled with joy.
Your desire to do my will
has brought you peace.

Day 13

"That's why he has made you king.
He knows that you will do what is fair and right."

1 Kings 10:9b

∿

God helped Solomon to know
right from wrong.
God will help me make good choices too.

GOD SAYS TO ME ...

I gave Solomon more wisdom
than any man on earth.
I gave him riches and fame.
I wanted Solomon
to use his gifts wisely
to help my people.
Use your gifts wisely too.

Day 14

"Asa did what was right in the eyes of the Lord.
That's what King David had done."

1 Kings 15:11

∾

Long ago, Asa learned a lesson from
others' mistakes. God, I can learn from mistakes.
I can do what is right the first time.

GOD SAYS TO ME ...

People turned away from me.
Even the kings made bad choices.
But I will call them back
again and again.
I will never stop trying.
I'm your loving God.
You are my people.

Day 15

"Then the woman said to Elijah, 'Now I know that
you are a man of God. I know that the message
you have brought from the Lord is true'."

1 Kings 17:24

∽

God helped Elijah.
He helped Elisha.
God will help me too.

GOD SAYS TO ME ...

Sometimes you are far away from me.

You cannot hear me say,

"I love you,"

But you will hear me

through my prophets.

They are my voice.

Listen.

Day 16

"Then I heard the voice of the Lord. He said,
'Who will I send? Who will go for us?'
I said, 'Here I am. Send me!'"

Isaiah 6:8

∽

God didn't give up on Isaiah.
God doesn't give up on anyone.
God will not give up on me!

GOD SAYS TO ME ...

I had a big plan.
The people did not listen
to my helper Isaiah.
So I kept trying.
I sent my Son to help them.
Now he is the hope of everyone.
My Son is your Savior too.

Day 17

"I will give you hope for the years to come."

Jeremiah 29:11

❧

God loved his people when they
made good or bad choices.
God always loves me too.

GOD SAYS TO ME ...

My love for you cannot
be measured.
It has no beginning
and never ends.
Reach out to me,
for I am right here beside you.
Believe in me
and have hope.

Day 18

"He does miraculous signs and wonders.
He does them in the heavens and on the earth.
He has saved Daniel from the power of the lions."

Daniel 6:27

Daniel trusted God
and God helped him.
I can trust in God too.

GOD SAYS TO ME …
I am God Almighty.
Great is my power.
I can do anything from making
the sun stand still to closing the
mouths of hungry lions.
Great is your trust in me.
I am a loving God
who cares for his people.

Day 19

"Then everyone God had
stirred up got ready to go."

Ezra 1:5a

❧

Long ago, God's people
promised to follow God.
I will follow God too.

GOD SAYS TO ME ...
From this day forward
you will be my temple—
not a temple of stone and rafters,
but a temple of people.
Go now and be my message
that the Creator of the
universe lives among you.

Day 20

"It's possible that you became queen
for a time just like this."

Esther 4:14b

God helped Esther do a hard job.
He helped her be brave.
God helps me be brave too.

GOD SAYS TO ME ...

Great was Esther's courage.
She helped rescue my people
from harm. She valued their
safety over her own.
Another one shall come soon.
His love will go on forever.
He will lay down his life to
save my people.
He laid down his life for you.

Day 21

"Come on. Let's rebuild the wall of Jerusalem."

Nehemiah 2:17

❧

Nehemiah knew God was
on his side.
God is on my side too.

GOD SAYS TO ME …

My temple is built
and my people worship
there in peace.
I led them back to my holy city
where they belong.
I am their God and they are my people.
You are my child too!
Welcome home.

Day 22

"Today in the town of David a Savior has been
born to you. He is Christ, the Lord."

Luke 2:11

God sent his Son to save all people.
I trust Jesus to help me too!

GOD SAYS TO ME ...

Today my Son has been born as a
human. Like you, he will laugh
and cry. Like you, he will know
the love and comfort of family
and friends. Like you, he will
experience sadness and pain.
Born to be your Savior, he will live
among you and bring you great joy.
He will be your hope and your salvation.

Day 23

"Jesus became wiser and stronger."
Luke 2:52a

∽

God's power shows through Jesus' work.
God's power is in me too.

GOD SAYS TO ME ...

Jesus is my Son.
You can see how much I love you
through his works and words.
I have remembered the promise
I made long ago, to send a Savior.
Together we show our love for
you and for all people.

Day 24

"I and the Father are one."

John 10:30

❧

Jesus was a teacher.
He taught many people about his Father.
He teaches me about his Father too.

GOD SAYS TO ME ...

Open your eyes and your ears.
You will soon understand
that Jesus is many things.
He is my Son. He is the Savior.
He is the teacher.
Learn about what love is by
listening to Jesus' words and
hearing about his work.

Day 25

"Then he took the children in his arms.
He put his hands on them and blessed them."

Mark 10:16

Jesus loved little children.
Jesus loves me too!

GOD SAYS TO ME …

To understand my kingdom
keep your faith simple
and just believe.
Love me with all of your heart
and love others.
Then my kingdom will be yours.

Day 26

"When these things begin to take place, stand up. Hold your head up with joy and hope. The time when you will be set free will be very close."

Luke 21:28

❧

Jesus died for our sins
so we can live in heaven with him.
I can live with him in heaven.

GOD SAYS TO ME ...

Together, my Son and I will change
your darkness to light.
We will change your sadness to joy.
Through Jesus, my kingdom
will live forever. Trust in us.
You have my promise:
the best is yet to come!

Day 27

"He is not here!
He has risen, just as he said he would!
Come and see the place where he was lying."

Matthew 28:6

∼

God gave Jesus new life.
He will give me new life.
I just need to ask.

GOD SAYS TO ME …

My Son is risen from the dead!
Share it with everyone.
Get ready to be filled
with the Holy Spirit!
I will send you strength
though the Holy Spirit. Tell everyone
the good news that Jesus has
saved the world. He has saved you too.

Day 28

"And you will be my witnesses from
one end of the earth to the other."

Acts 1:8b

❧

God gives his followers the Holy Spirit.
The Holy Spirit can live in me too.

GOD SAYS TO ME ...

The Holy Spirit lives in you.
His power helps you be brave.
Tell the world the Savior has come.
Be filled with joy.
God help spread the
Good News!

Day 29

" ... in the name of the Father and of
the Son and of the Holy Spirit."
Matthew 28:19b

❦

Paul believed in Jesus and
Jesus helped him work.
I believe in Jesus too.

GOD SAYS TO ME ...
Please remember
I will take care of you
and watch over you,
just like I took care of
Paul and Silas.
Powerful and wonderful things
will happen when you
follow me.

Day 30

"I have fought the good fight.
I have finished the race. I have kept
the faith."
2 Timothy 4:7

Paul worked to give God glory.
I can give God glory too.

GOD SAYS TO ME ...

Do not be afraid my child.
I will be with you forever and always.
I have a plan for you—
a great and grand plan
for your future.
Trust in me. I am your Father.

Day 31

"Look! I am coming soon!"
Revelation 22:7

❧

God loves me. I am a child of Jesus.
I will be with him in heaven …
Forever!

GOD SAYS TO ME …

Wait patiently, my child,
for I will come again.
I will remember my promise and
my kingdom will come again.
On that day, there will be singing
in the streets and rejoicing in heaven.
Peace and joy and goodness will
replace war, sadness, and evil.
All will be well.

MY SALVATION PRAYER

Father God, I am sorry.
I ask you to forgive me of all my sins.
I confess with my mouth that
Jesus Christ is Lord.
I know and believe in my heart
that Jesus Christ died and
God raised him from the dead.
Jesus, please come into my life.
Be my Lord and Savior.
Amen.

The ABCs of Salvation

All people are sinners.
Romans 3:23

Everyone has sinned. No one measures up to God's glory.

The **Bible** is God's word of love and salvation.
John 20:31

But these are written down so that you may believe that Jesus is the Christ, the Son of God. If you believe this, you will have life because you belong to him.

The **condition** of sinners is serious.
2 Thessalonians 2:12

Many will not believe the truth. They will take pleasure in evil. They will be judged.

Christ **died** to save sinners.
Romans 5:8

But here is how God has shown his love for us. While we were still sinners, Christ died for us.

(E)

Everyone who believes will have **eternal** life.
John 3:16

God loved the world so much that he gave his one and only Son. Anyone who believes in him will not die but will have eternal life.

(F)

You are saved through **faith**.
Romans 1:17

The good news shows how God makes people right with himself. From beginning to end, becoming right with God depends on a person's faith. It is written, "Those who are right with God will live by faith."

(G)

Good works will not save you.
Ephesians 2:8-9

God's grace has saved you because of your faith in Christ. Your salvation doesn't come from anything you do. It is God's gift. It is not based on anything you have done. No one can brag about earning it.

(H)

Hell and punishment are waiting for those who don't believe.
2 Thessalonians 1:8-9

He will punish those who don't know God. He will punish those who don't obey the good news about our Lord Jesus. They will be destroyed forever. They will be shut out of heaven. They will never see the glory of the Lord's power.

I

Nothing is **impossible** for God.
Luke 1:37

Nothing is impossible with God.

J

There is **joy** in heaven over one sinner who repents.
Luke 15:10

I tell you, it is the same in heaven. There is joy in heaven over one sinner who turns away from sin.

K

If you trust God, he will **keep** you from sin.
Jude 1:24

Give praise to the One who is able to keep you from falling into sin. He will bring you into his heavenly glory without any fault. He will bring you there with great joy.

L

God **loves** sinners and wants to save them.
John 3:16

God loved the world so much that he gave his one and only Son. Anyone who believes in him will not die but will have eternal life.

M

God has **mercy** on unbelievers.
Romans 11:32

**God has found everyone guilty of not obeying him.
So now he can have mercy on everyone.**

N

Jesus is the only **name** by which you can be saved.
Acts 4:12

**You can't be saved by believing in anyone else. God has given
us no other name under heaven that will save us.**

O

You show God you love him by **obeying** his commandments.
1 John 5:3

**Here is what it means to love God. It means that we obey
his commands. And his commands are not hard to obey.**

P

God is **patient** with unbelievers.
2 Peter 3:9

**The Lord is not slow to keep his promise. He is not slow in the
way some people understand it. He is patient with you. He doesn't
want anyone to be destroyed. Instead, he wants all people to turn
away from their sins.**

Those who don't believe should **quickly** decide to follow Jesus.
2 Corinthians 6:2

He says, "When I showed you my favor, I heard you. On the day I saved you, I helped you." I tell you, now is the time God shows his favor. Now is the day he saves.

Christians have a **reason** to rejoice.
Luke 10:20

But do not be glad when the evil spirits obey you.
Instead, be glad that your names are written in heaven.

S

The Bible, the **Scriptures**, can teach you how to be saved.
2 Timothy 3:15

You have known the Holy Scriptures ever since you were a little child. They are able to teach you how to be saved by believing in Christ Jesus.

T

You should give **thanks** to God for the wonderful gift of salvation.
2 Corinthians 9:15

Let us give thanks to God for his gift. It is so great that no one can tell how wonderful it really is!

The Holy Spirit helps us **understand** God's Word.
1 Corinthians 2:12

We have not received the spirit of the world. We have received the Spirit who is from God. The Spirit helps us understand what God has freely given us.

Jesus has gained **victory** over death for you.
1 Corinthians 15:54

In fact, that is going to happen. What does not last will be dressed with what lasts forever. What dies will be dressed with what does not die. Then what is written will come true. It says, "Death has been swallowed up. It has lost the battle."

W

Whoever calls on Jesus will be saved.
Acts 2:21

Everyone who calls on the name of the Lord will be saved.

Y

God loves **you** so much he calls you his child.
1 John 3:1

How great is the love the Father has given us so freely! Now we can be called children of God. And that's what we really are! The world doesn't know us because it didn't know him.

Check out this First Ever Storybook Bible written by Max Lucado

The Story for Children, A Storybook Bible
Max Lucado, Randy Frazee, and Karen Davis Hill

With sweeping brush strokes, God painted his creation across the emptiness. "Let there be light," he called into the darkness, and a sweep of brightness blazed across the blank canvas.

The Story for Children isn't just another collection of Bible stories—it's The Story— the big picture of God's enormous love for his children! Presented by bestselling author and pastor Max Lucado with Randy Frazee and Karen Hill, these 48 pivotal stories show how God has a great, grand, and glorious vision, beginning with Creation and ending with the promise that Jesus is coming again. Each story is personalized with "God's Message" and accompanied by vibrant illustrations from accomplished artist Fausto Bianchi that help bring the Bible to life for readers young and old.

Ideal for children ages 4–7.

The Story Trading Cards: For Elementary

Grades 3 and up

This set of trading cards was created to correspond to *The Story for Children.* Each card depicts a scene from the Bible story with the Bible verse for that lesson on the back.

Available in stores and online!

ZONDERVAN®
.com

New Deluxe Edition Featuring Audio Narration by Max Lucado!

The Story for Children, a Storybook Bible Deluxe Edition
Max Lucado, Randy Frazee, and Karen Davis Hill

The Story for Children isn't just another collection of Bible stories—it's The Story—the big picture of God's enormous love for his children! Presented by bestselling author and pastor Max Lucado with Randy Frazee and Karen Hill, these 48 pivotal stories show how God has a great, grand, and glorious vision, beginning with creation and ending with the promise that Jesus is coming again. Each story is personalized with "God's Message" and accompanied by vibrant illustrations from accomplished artist Fausto Bianchi that help bring the Bible to life for readers young and old.

This beautifully crafted deluxe edition, with enhanced audio CDs narrated by Max Lucado, is a wonderful gift and sure to become a family treasure.

Available in stores and online!

ZONDERVAN®
.com

New Full-Text Bible for Kids That Shows God's Great Love for His Children

The Story for Children Bible, NIrV
Max Lucado, Randy Frazee, and Karen Davis Hill

The Story for Children Bible, NIV is a large-print Bible for children ages six to nine with 32 beautiful full-color pictures highlighting important Bible stories with Scripture reference. The stories end with "God's Message," sharing with children God's great love for us. Each "message" was written by beloved pastor and bestselling author Max Lucado along with Randy Frazee and Karen Davis Hill.

Features include:
- 32 pages of full-color Bible story illustrations
- Large print (12-point) type for easy reading
- Book introductions
- Dictionary-concordance to explain key Bible words
- 8 pages of full-color maps to show where Bible events happened
- Presentation page for personalization and gift giving

Available in stores and online!

ZONDERVAN®
.com

A Storybook Bible for Young Children about God's Great Love!

The Story for Little Ones
Discover the Bible in Pictures

Now children can experience God's great love story! *The Story for Little One*s is filled with vibrant illustrations and simple text that bring 31 pivotal Bible stories, including Creation, David and Goliath, and the birth of Jesus to life for children. At the end of each story, a simple message will help children personalize and remember the greatest story ever told.
Ideal for children ages 2–5.

The Story Trading Cards: For Preschool

Pre-K through Grade 2

This set of trading cards was created to correspond with *The Story for Little Ones.* Each card depicts a scene from the Bible story with the Bible verse for that lesson on the back.

Available in stores and online!

ZONDERVAN®
.com